WHY CAN'T I SELL?

GET SALES IN YOUR FITNESS BUSINESS

More clients
Less work

Thank you

More Clients Less Work sales tool kit for the health and fitness industry.

Primarily focused on independents and small to medium business.
This has been built from learning from the big box players in the fitness industry and I want to share these tools with people in the fitness industry who wouldn't normally have access to this information.

I believe all people should exercise and be healthy and this gives the fitness industry the right tools to help those who need help.

With your feedback I can make this tool;
1. User friendly
2. Easy to read and easy to use
3. Relevant
4. Effective

At present it is a list of scripts for day to day use.

What are your thoughts to make this better?

I understand you are busy and any time you take to look at this is appreciated.

For collaboration on ideas and thoughts post them on the Facebook community more clients for less work
https://www.facebook.com/moreclientslesswork

Send any feedback on this book to jade.philippe@mail.com with the subject e-book feedback.

moreclientslesswork.com

Thank you again,

Jade Philippe

Moreclientslesswork.com

Letter to the reader

The following scripts have been used by Big Box players in the Fitness industry for years. These have been developed over time to create the best possible practice. You can used these tools as a guide or verbatim.

I would always encourage you to follow the rule of 21 – that is; do something 21 times consistently to form a habit. I have personally used these and trained 100s of people in these practices and have seen the results over a period of over 12 years.

I have studied from numerous training organisations and have adapted them over my experience to bring you the product you see today.

For more specific tools and training on the following scripts you can visit my website at www.moreclientslesswork.com

Also feel free to grab free content from the homepage.

Yours in fitness,

Jade Philippe

Don't let your learning lead to knowledge, let your learning lead to action

TABLE OF CONTENTS

More clients Less work

Contents

Accept what is useful, reject what is useless add to it what is specifically your own

Bruce Lee

Goal Setting

Let's start at the very beginning; it's a very good place to start. Or at least that's what Fraulein Maria taught us in the Sound of Music. If you haven't asked yourself yet, why am I here? Why am I reading this? What hope did I expect from this? These are good questions and should be the starting point and building blocks to understand your goals.

I want to use a framework to help you define your goals, be clear about them, understand them, articulate them and most importantly act upon them. One of my favourite quotes is;

Don't let your learning lead to knowledge, let it lead to action

Goal setting the 5 step process

1. Imagination – dream big, all avenues of life

    a. How big can I dream?

    b. Fearless – What can I do if I know I cannot fail?

2. Intention – why is this important to me?

    a. Why is 80% - Focus on where you want to go

    b. How is 20% - the why is more important question

    c. Don't let the dream die in the detail

3. Attention – Focus, immerse myself in things daily that will work

    a. Review goals daily

    b. Do the highest priorities 1st

    c. Write them down

4. New direction – follow the direction, continue in the direction

5. Creation - celebrate

Goal setting - Let's put it into practice

What are my values?
Write your answers down and order them.

- _____
- _____
- _____

What do you want to get out of this?
Write your answers down and order them.

- _____
- _____
- _____

What are my goals? Brainstorm all areas of life including work, social, health, family, hobbies.
Don't let the dream die in the detail

- _____
- _____
- _____

Next to your goals define what length of time you want them completed by; 1 month, 3 months or 6 months. I like working in short term goal, makes them actionable and real.

Once you have defined your length of goal, prioritise them, ask yourself, "If I had to get this goal done and nothing else, would I be happy?

First work on your 1 month goals, define them like this;

Goal 1: Achieve 1000 Facebook likes by November 1st, 2016
Why is this important to me?
This will help to build a social platform to promote my business to with future product offerings. This will help to establish long term success in fitness

Notice the Why in the above question drives the behavior. Having a clear understanding of your why will keep you motivated to achieve your goals.

If you haven't done goal setting before, STOP what you are doing and do it now. No time like the present.

Success by Definition

What is success? What does success look like? How do we define success? OK, now that I have written it a few times, even the word is starting to look funny.

I like to define success from my WHY. My why is determined by <u>goal setting</u>. We need a reminder of our goals so we know what success looks like. If you are like me you have defined your goals by your priorities, by what is important to you, there are a number of sources you can use, I like Dream lining by Time Ferris and there a number of great available goal setting tools.

Once we establish our goals, we need to measure our performance towards our goals, like the old management line;

If you can't measure it you can't manage it

If we use the example of a client that is trying to lose weight, we can easily put them on the scales, see where they are currently and where they want to get to their goal number and we ask them why they want to achieve this. From here we simply focus on an improved eating plan and get them burning more calories and we put them on the road to success. We measure them at set times, encourage them on their progress and voilà! They achieve their goals.

So what does you success look like? We need to define it, into manageable, workable daily tasks that we complete to get us towards our goal. If it is as simple as a financial goal, what is the number? Start with your end figure, break it down into monthly, weekly or daily figures. What tasks do you need to do daily to get daily goal figure. In most instances the daily figure is not that scary and you have potentially done it before. Now it is about execution and repetition towards this goal.

Each day come with a clear agenda of what you need to do today to be successful. Speak to that business, call that client, make contact with that prospect and take action. The more you do it the less daunting it will become.

Perfect Prospect

Who knows the feeling when we just wasted a lead? You hear a call and you cringe... wasted opportunity for you and for the prospect. Do we know how much courage it may have taken that person to call in and it's over in the blink of an eye, with not even a phone number recorded. No one is perfect but let's imagine for a second we could create a perfect prospect. Someone who says;

- I want to exercise to lose weight
- I need to train 4x per week
- I need your help and support
- I have friends I want to train with
- I need to achieve my goals by a goal date

It sounds great, so let's control what we can control to create our own perfect prospects. Have you ever run in to a friend of a friend at a party or function and inevitably they say, "So what do you do?" You respond with, "I work at a gym" (or some derivative) and you are immediately greeted with, so tell me;

- How do I lose this fat gut?
- How do I get a 6 pack?
- I want massive pecs!
- What's the secret to getting shredded?

We are non-threatening, we are the solution and our advice is offered up free. We become their hero and moments later they are offering to throw dollars our way to help. This is what we do to create our perfect prospect, we ask the right questions to gain the right insight to best help them. The following outlines, role-plays or scripts are designed to give you the best way to get the information you need to best help them and create your own clients. Let's go and create More Clients for Less Work.

Speaking the same language

This basis of this book is for you to use in your very own business and you may call people different things in your workplace, for transparency I am defining people in roles and will denote them as the role they function in, not necessarily their position.

When in the role of reception I will call the person reception, this role may be being performed by a manager or PT or sales person. You can rename them at your discretion.

So the following roles and terms will be in the text;

Reception – a person performing the role of receptionist

Sales – a person performing a sales function

Prospect – A prospective client or member, not yet paying you money

Walk In – An unsolicited lead, a type of prospect that is considering buying your product that has walked into your business

Phone In - An unsolicited lead, a type of prospect that is considering buying your product that has called your business via the phone

Lead – a name and phone number; with the intention to make contact

I will talk through the theory of the scripting and delivery. Take notes; think about the why they were written in this way, what information and needs are we trying to establish? What goals does the prospect have? How do we best help?

Get you priorities in order

Let's look at the world of to do lists. This is a great place to organise what you will and will not do. You know when you feel you have been productive and got stuff done, that's the space we want to live in daily.

So what are your high impact tasks? What, when done yields an outcome? When is the best time for this to take place. Outline the key priorities you feel must be done on a given day, I like working with 2 or 3 high impact tasks, things that will take under 30 minutes each to do in completion. Focus on 1 at a time and get them done early, prior to 11am ideally.

Feel free to write down as many things on your to do list as you like, preferably the day before action needs to take place. Review your list and prioritise it in a ranking scale; high, med and low. Next decide who needs to do it, must it be done by me or can I delegate it? You can delegate based on better use of your time as it may be time consuming or someone else is simply better at it and will get a better result.

Next review your list and decide if the task needs to be done at all or if the time spent on it is worth the effort. In essence, review redundant tasks. Clear your mind of things taking up space and consider where that energy could be better spent on your business or a better outcome for your clients. Is what you are doing helping you get more clients for less work?

Look at your to do list as stepping stones towards your overall goal, by taking these steps am I getting closer to my goal or is it a distraction? Decide if I got just these things done on my to do list I would be productive. Don't confuse busy with productive. Busy sounds like we are important or effective, BUT check the results. Look at the scorecard, is this busyness effecting real world results? When people are working with or for you, help them navigate their to do lists with the same end goal in mind. Question what you are doing and don't fall into the trap of doing it, because it has always been done that way.

You control your to do list, it does not control you.

RECEPTION SCRIPTS

1ˢᵗ impressions count

Making a great first impression, we have roughly 7 seconds to make a first impression and how many chances do you reckon we get at it? Yep you got it, 1. So it's pretty important we do a good job of it, wouldn't you say? From my experience I would tell sales people, PTs and customer service staff I can almost guarantee you have won or lost the sale within the first 7 seconds. We need to consider a number of things when making a great first impression;

Face to face	Over the phone
• How we look	• Answer in 3 rings
• Do we smell good?	• Consistent friendly greeting
• Appropriately groomed	• Listen, respond and direct
• Are we smiling	• Smile – you can hear it
• Do we want to be here	• Interested in them
• Look at them in the eye	• Follow the script
• Shake their hand	•
• Receive them as a guest	•

Once we have our game face on we are ready to greet the world and create happy clients that keep coming back.

moreclientslesswork.com

What are your keys to make a great first impression?

_____

_____

_____

_____

_____

_____

RECEPTION INCOMING CALL GREETING

RECEPTION: Thank you for calling Business Health clubs, this is Receptionist, how can I help you?

Prospect: *asks question*

RECEPTION: Yes sure, we can definitely help you out with that, my name is Receptionist who am I speaking to?

Phone in: Bob

RECEPTION: Great **Bob** and are you a member?

If Yes   *Service oriented call, help out*   RECEPTION : Is there any other way I can help?

If No   RECEPTION: You've called through to location, is that the best club for you?

Is the membership for yourself?   **Will you be training with a friend or partner?**

Have you been to our club before?

What things are you particularly interested in?

Fantastic, well (name) that sounds great I'd love to invite you to the club so we can have a chat about your program and the types of results you were looking at achieving.

Let me see, I have **today** available at _____ or would _____ suit you better?

Well thanks for calling let me grab your details your full name phone number.

Do you know how to get here and where to park?

Really looking forward to seeing you in club (name), my name is Receptionist I'll see you soon.

Prospect objection

OK, well I am here to help, have you got access to the web or would you prefer to pop into the club?

Our website is Business.com from there you can grab a pass, find out about our clubs or join, what were you looking at doing?

RECEPTION: (Smile, make eye contact)

Reception walk in greeting

Walk in refers to unsolicited prospect – who is considering buying your service

All non-members to be welcomed with this greeting

RECEPTION: (Smile, make eye contact)

Hi, welcome to the club. How can I help today?

Prospect: I just wanted to find out prices / find out about membership etc...

RECEPTION: Sure! My pleasure... <u>we'd</u> love to give you all the information about the club, my name is ....who am I speaking too?

Prospect: Bob

Great **Bob,** I'll just get you to fill in our **guest** register and who is your appointment with?

Prospect: I don't have an appointment OR I just want to know prices

RECEPTION: Did you want to speak to someone or just get started?

RECEPTION: Sure Bob, I'll grab the best person to help you with that, grab a seat in our members lounge. I'll just get you to fill this out, (hand over needs analysis) just the **front page** thanks.

Please take a seat; someone will be out to help shortly.

Call Sales *"Hi there, we have a **guest** here who would like to get started."*

IF objection;

We just do this to save you time and for O, H and S reasons, you understand. Just the front page, grab a seat and someone will be with you shortly, thanks.

RECEPTION GREETING IN PERSON

Hi, welcome to the club. How can I help today?

Prospect: I just wanted to find out prices / find out about membership etc...

RECEPTION: Sure! My pleasure... <u>we'd</u> love to give you all the information about the club, my name is ....and your name?

Prospect: Bob

Great **Bob,** I'll just get you to fill in our **guest** register and who is your appointment with?

Prospect: I don't have an appointment OR I have been speaking to (Sales name)

RECEPTION: Great well I am here to help, have you seen the club before?
Take through needs analysis sales process

How did you go? Club's pretty great hey?   *Add specific feature of your club*
Let me show you the best way to get started   *direct to website/ tablet*

Answer any questions relating to the prospects queries to the best of your ability
Navigate through the website or tablet until you reach the pricing options

RECEPTION: We have 2 suitable options this or that which would you prefer?

Prospect: that

RECEPTION: Great, welcome to the Club.

We have these amazing VIP passes for new members; it allows you to invite 10 of your best friends who you would like to spoil with access to the Health club. Simply pop down the 10 friends you would like to invite on the VIP list.

NLP – Neuro Linguistic Programming

Ever walked into a retail store and been asked by the shop assistant, "***Hi can I help?***" to which our instant response is, "***No thanks, just looking.***" Or walk past a colleague in the corridor and it's, "***Hi, how are you?***" and the response, "***Good thanks and you?***" This is all said while still walking past with no interest in the actual response to "***How are you?***"

Why is this? Why do we respond in this way, the long answer is NLP – Neuro Linguistic Programming, meaning;

Neuro – the brain

Linguistic – Language

Programming – automated responses due to habit

NLP – The way we respond to common situations and questions, that we have been programmed to respond to in a certain way.

So once we understand the concept of NLP, we start to see in ourselves and others; pre-programmed responses. If we observe this we can start to build a resource that says, if I say "X" someone will respond in this way and if I don't they will respond in another.

The key is to remove the questions and statements that dictate a negative NLP response and add questions that elicit a positive NLP response. This will cause our prospect to think.

So how do we do this? In a nutshell, follow the script! Each question has its meaning and its order and when we put it together we create best practice with best outcomes.

NLP is not just limited to language, it is inbuilt into our body language too and body language NLP cues have big impact. Look at your closest friends and family, you will notice you share similar body language traits; this is evidenced by massive rapport and trust. Massive rapport and trust, that's what I want with my clients... do you?

Outline the positive and negative NLP language that you or your business displays

_____

_____

_____

_____

_____

_____

SALES SCRIPTS

OVERVIEW PHONE CALL

I will outline the building blocks to making a great call. I have broken the call into areas with key questions for a desired outcome.

INTRO

- Looking at getting started on some training?
- Been to club before?
- Live/work in area? (convenient)
- How did you hear about us? (Friend train here?)

NEEDS

- WHAT – interested in?
- WHAT – results?
- WHERE – 2-3 areas work on?
- WHEN – achieve by? (optional – depending on rapport)

BOOKING THE CALL

- Training – how many days per week?
- Training – before or after work?
- What days are best?
- When would suit you best – today/tomorrow?
- Afternoon/evening?
- 2 times specific to when they would be training

WRAP UP

- Mobile no
- Most people bring a friend_____name

- Directions
- Confirm - goals, info, time, name

Example enquiry card to tick:

ENQUIRY CARD							
DATE:							
NAME:							
MOBILE:							
LIVE/WORK LOCALLY:							
INTERESTED IN:	CARDIO		WEIGHTS	CLASSES		12 WEEK CHALLENGE	YOGAL/PILATES	OTHER:
GOALS:	LOSE WEIGHT		TONE UP	TRIM DOWN		GAIN MUSCLE	OTHER:	
2-3 AREAS:							
CHAT DATE & TIME:							
REFERRAL:							

BASIC PHONE SCRIPT

Incoming call

Reception *"Good morning/Afternoon/Evening – thank-you for calling Business Health clubs (suburb) this is (name)"*

Prospect: Answer

Reception *"Sure, my pleasure, We'd love to give you all the information about the club, I'm (name), who am I speaking with?"*

Prospect answer

Reception *Thanks (name) let me put you through to (name) and he/she will be able to give you all the information about the club!"*

Reception – put's it through to SALES and give's the SALES prospects name before transferring through.

SALES *" Hi (prospect) I'm (SALES's name) how are you today?"*

Prospect – answer

SALES *"Fantastic – (reception) mentioned you'd like to know a little bit about the club.*
So you're looking at getting started on some training?"

Prospect – answer

SALES: *Sure – my pleasure, I'd love to give you all the information about our club/training –you've actually called at the best time as we have some fantastic offers on at the moment... Tell me (name) have you been down to the club before?*

Prospect - Answer

SALES: *"Do you live or work in the area?" (are we convenient for you?)*

Prospect – answer

SALES: *"Fantastic! And how did you find out about us? Do you know anyone that trains here?"*

Prospect – answer

(If they know someone who trains there – ask their name and other rapport building questions)

SALES: *"What types of things are you particularly interested in? Would it be more cardio, weights, group fitness classes, personal training or our 12 week challenge program?"*

Prospect – answer

SALES: *"Fantastic – with your exercise program what type of results are you looking for? Would it be more toning up, trimming down, building muscle, weight loss?"*

Prospect – answer

SALES: *"Fantastic!*

SALES: *"Where are 2-3 areas that you most want to focus on?"*
(Great, most people say that! We have plenty of fantastic programs that can help you achieve that – I can fill you in more on that when you come down)"

SALES: *"Ok (name), I'd love to invite you down to the club so we can more of a Call about (insert goals) and how we can assist you with that."*

SALES: *"How many days per week would you be looking at training?"*
Prospect – answer

SALES: *"Excellent – that will definitely get you on your way! Will you be training before or after work?"*

Prospect – answer

SALES: *"What days would suit you best to train?"*

Prospect – answer

SALES: *"Fantastic! When is best for you to come down – would today or tomorrow suit you best?"*

Prospect – answer

SALES: *"Great – afternoon/evening?"*

Prospect – answer

SALES: *"Excellent – you're really lucky, I've still got a couple of spaces available – would 5.20 or 6.40 suit you best?"*

Prospect – answer

SALES: *"Great- now just in case we need to make some changes can I grab your mobile no?"*

Prospect – answer

SALES: *"Most people feel more comfortable training with a friend/family member – who would you like to bring with you?"*

Prospect – answer

SALES: *"Excellent – do they have similar goals to you?"*

Prospect – answer

SALES: *"Great – let me check, do you know how to get here? I'll also send it to you in a text."*

Prospect – answer

SALES: *"Fantastic – ok (name) what I am going to do is work on some information specific to (goal listed) and Call with some of the trainers here to work out what is going to maximise your results and we can go through that when you come down! Like I said early, we have some fantastic offers on – So I'll go through that with you when you come down to the club! So just come to reception at (insert time day) and ask for me (name) and I look forward to showing you (and friend) how we can help you with (goals)! See you then, bye!*

Outsourced leads

such as LED trailer signs, competitions set up / text message posters

The theory behind the call is that you need to qualify them and do a mini needs analysis so you can generate rapport and build a relationship so they are keen to meet you and keen to see you or the facility.

SALES: Hi is this Amanda?

Prospect - Yes

SALES: It's Jade calling from Business Health Clubs in Adelaide how are you today?

Prospect - Answer

SALES: The reason for my call is that you filled out an entry form at Subway for a health club membership competition – which is fantastic! So you're looking at getting started on some training?

Qualifying & Rapport building questions:

1. Fantastic! So (name) Do you live or work in the Adelaide area? **(LIVE)**

2. Have you been to our fitness club before?

3. If you were to start a health and fitness program what sort of things would you like to work on, say, fitness, toning, strength, body shaping etc? **(RESULTS)**

4. How many times will you train per week? **(TRAIN)**

5. And finally, what sort of things do you see yourself using at our gym to help you lose weight/ get shredded/ bulk up, would it be classes, personal training, an individual weights program? (You'll need to insert 3 things that would help them achieve the result they desire)

6. If the Prospect says classes then respond with "great, we've got this awesome class called PUMP and it works your entire body firming up your muscles. It's great for all fitness levels as you choose the weight you want to lift. Does that sound like something you'd be interested in?

7. Great and it you enjoyed your training would you consider continuing after the 5 days? **(QUALIFY)**

SALES: Ok, the best thing for us to do now is arrange a time so we can help you get started on your training and I can take you around the club to show you all the things you can do to help you tone up. Would day time or evening better for you? Today or tomorrow? Ok, let me check I've got a time at 10.30 or 11.40, which is better for you?

SALES: If anything comes up between now and then I'll give you my number so you can call me, its _____ and my name is Jade.

SALES: Do you know where our new club is? It's located at.....

SALES: Most members feel more comfortable if they bring someone along with them, who would you like to bring? Oh, and what's their name?

SALES: Fantastic, I'll see you and Emily on Saturday at 10.30, have a great day.

Automated Lead management system such as Gym Sales, will send a confirmation text to the person prior to the meeting this will aid in prospect arriving to the appointment.

OUTBOUND CALLS

Proactive outbound contact is key to growing your business; we need to capitalize in this area to take us from zero to hero. 1 such form is Referrals.

Referrals are key to business success – 70% and more of our members come from referrals when done properly, so we want to be good at this. Did you know you are 3 times more likely to achieve your goals when training with a friend? Because they are referral you want to link how the referral connection is made and draw on this during your conversation. Using qualifying questions during referral generation will help aid in your referral calls. Let's consider 2 scenarios;

1. Referred prospect 1; lives 200km away from your location, has a gym membership already is loving it there, doesn't really know the referrer and hasn't spoken to them in years
2. Referred prospect 2; lives close by, works close by, is best friends with existing member, has been talking about training together, wants to start straight away

In the examples above, we clearly want prospect 2, so we help create this by asking the right questions when gaining referrals from existing members.

Qualify referrals with these steps;

- Relationship - How do you know this person?
- Live – so your friend lives or works close by?
- Train - Are they training currently?
- Results – What type of results do you think they want? Similar to you or different?
- Qualify – Who would most likely want to come down and train with you?

Referral outbound call option 1

Hi this is _____(SALES name) from Business fitness, how are you today?

Your friend _____(new member) just got started at the club with us, did they tell you about it?? Well he/she's said that you were keen on getting started on some training?

Well the great thing is _____ (new member) has organised for you to receive a free 3 day membership so you can come down and try out the club with them – that's great isn't it!

Qualifying questions for referrals

1. "Tell me (name), do you work or live in the area?" **(LIVE)**

2. Have you been to a fitness club before?

3. What sort of results would you be looking for? **(RESULTS)**

4. What can you see yourself doing? You may need to prompt them with a few ideas such as classes, weights, treadmill etc…

5. Where are 2-3 areas you most want to work on?

6. Fantastic, we definitely have some programs that can help you with that….

7. How many days per week would you like to train? **(TRAIN)**

8. What time of the day do you like to train? Morning, afternoon, evening?

9. "If you enjoy your trial membership, would you consider continuing?" **(QUALIFY)**

Great! Well the best thing to do is organise for you to come down and use your complimentary membership, is tonight or tomorrow better? (Depending on the time of day they said they want to train).

When you come on down, I'll run through a bit of exercise history with you and show you through the club and how we can help you!

Also, we have some great membership specials on at the moment so I'll run you through those as well.

Also_____(name), most members feel more comfortable training with a friend and we can extend that pass to someone else as well, who would you like to bring with you?

So you know how to get to the club?

Fantastic, I look forward to seeing you and _____(referral name) at __(time), just ask for me _____(SALES name) and I look forward to meeting you and showing you more of what Business has to offer!

Points to remember on script

Qualifying questions are deigned to create the types of prospect you want

It builds a template of when they would be training and the results they are likely to achieve

By asking for a friend to come with the referral we create 2 appointments and 2 opportunities to sell

WEB LEADS

OUT-GOING CALL SCRIPTS

In your business you need to do what you can to get incoming leads, generally speaking when I say a lead I mean a person's name and phone number. It can also mean a Facebook friend, a name and email or a connection on Linked In, etc. You can have a good website that creates you paid or organic (non-paid) leads. You can subscribe to paid lead delivery services, such as GoodGymGuide. Create online incentives for people; clients, members and non-members to give you their details, including;

- Competition and prizes
- Free-content, such as nutrition advice, training advice gym programs
- Free pass, complimentary group fitness class, PT session or small group session, etc.

Link your website page to your Facebook or Instagram page to engage with your members or potential clients. Depending on how much you understand this world, you can always hire a professional to create a better ranked Google listed page. The key is without leads, you run out of puff. Engage people that like this space and get them to do it for you. Understand how many leads you need to survive by using a key metric tool, such as your lead to sale ratio, back on track calculator or similar. As with many things, sales is a numbers game, if you understand your key metric or key performance indicator being your lead to sale ratio you will know exactly what you need to break even, then to smash your goals.

Lead to sale ratio is, a collection of Key Performance indicators (KPI), including;

1. Lead to contact ratio – How many leads you need to make contact with someone
2. Contact to Appointment ratio – How many contacts it takes for you to make 1 appointment

3. Show ratio – How many appointments you make compared to how many people you see
4. Close ratio – The number of people you see compared to number of sales

The culmination of these 4 KPIs will give you a lead to sale ratio. Once you know how much profit each sale gives you, you will calculate how many sales you need to break even then using this KPI how many leads you require. You can measure these stats a number of ways, my preferred way is using a lead management tool called GymSales.net tell them Jade Philippe sent you. I personally endorse this program because I used it and it is the best I've seen so far. This tool will help you manage leads, make phone calls, send emails and texts and provide it in a user-friendly, visually appealing environment.

WEB LEAD FOLLOW UP CALL

SALES: "Hi, this is (SALES name) from Business health clubs is (prospect name) available please?"

SALES: "Hi (name) how are you today?"

SALES: "Great! I see that you have enquired about getting started on some training?"

Prospect - answer

SALES: "Fantastic -you've actually enquired at the best time as we have some fantastic offers on at the moment – Tell me (name) do you live or work in the area?" (Are we convenient for you?) **(LIVE)**

Prospect – answer

SALES: "Great! And how did you find out about us? Do you know anyone that trains here?"

Prospect – answer

(If they know someone who trains there – ask their name and other rapport building questions)

SALES: "Excellent – you mentioned that you are interested in (insert results from internet lead and ask questions about it) which is something we can definitely help you with! Do you have 2-3 areas that you most want to work on?" **(RESULTS)**

(Great, most people say that! We have plenty of fantastic programs that can help you achieve that – I can fill you in more on that when you come down)"

Prospect – answer

SALES: "And if you enjoyed your 3/5/7 day membership, would you consider continuing?" **(QUALIFY)**

Prospect - answer

SALES: "Ok (name), I'd love to invite you down to the club so we can more of a Call about (insert goals) and how we can assist you with that."

Prospect - answer

SALES: "How many days per week would you be looking at training?" **(TRAIN)**

Prospect – answer

SALES: "Excellent – that will definitely get you on your way! Will you be training before or after work?"

Prospect – answer

SALES: "What days would suit you best to train?"

Prospect – answer

SALES: "Fantastic! When is best for you to come down – would today or tomorrow suit you best?"

Prospect – answer

SALES: "Great – afternoon/evening?"

Prospect – answer

SALES: "Excellent – you're really lucky, I've still got a couple of spaces available – would 5.20 or 6.40 suit you best?"

Prospect – answer

SALES: "Great- now just in case we need to make some changes can I grab your mobile no?"

Prospect – answer

SALES: "Most people feel more comfortable training with a friend/family member – who would you like to bring with you?"

Prospect – answer

SALES: "Excellent – do they have similar goals to you?"

Prospect – answer

SALES: "Great – let me check, do you know how to get here? I'll also send it to you in a text."

Prospect – answer

SALES: "Fantastic – ok (name) what I am going to do is work on some information specific to (goal listed) and Call with some of the trainers here to work out what is going to maximise your results and we can go through that when you come down!

Like I said earlier, we have some fantastic promotional offers at the moment - I'll go through that with you when you come down to the club! So just come to reception at (insert time day) and ask for me (name) and I look forward to showing you (and friend) how we can help you with (goals)! See you then, bye!

NEW LEAD SCRIPT

SALES: Hi Emily, this is Jade from Business health clubs (suburb), how are you today?

Prospect – well thanks!

SALES: Great! You might remember the other day we met on Chapel street and you were interested in some training weren't you (tie down)

Prospect – answer

SALES: Well I thought I better give you a buzz so we could Call more about your training, you wanted to (insert goals) lose some weight/tone up, didn't you?

Prospect – answer

SALES: Fantastic, and you live in the Prahran area don't you? **(LIVE)**

Prospect – yes South Yarra

SALES: Great! So it's nice and convenient for you isn't it? So what sort of training are you looking at doing – was it more cardio, or weights, group fitness classes? (list examples)

Prospect – some classes and maybe some cardio

SALES: Ok excellent! By doing group fitness classes and cardio – how much weight are you looking to lose?

Prospect – about 5kg

SALES: Great – we can definitely help you with that – and where are the 2-3 main areas of your body you most want to focus on and lose weight/tone up? **(RESULTS)**

Prospect – tummy, hips and thighs

SALES: Ok, Emily, why is it important for you to tone up/lose weight from your tummy, hips and thighs?

Prospect – So I can fit back into my old jeans

ENSURE THAT YOU DO NOT MOVE ON UNTIL YOU HAVE THE PAIN. Other questions to use where the opportunity presents itself are:

- How is that a problem for you?

moreclientslesswork.com

- How does not fitting into your jeans make you feel?

SALES: Do you have something special coming up for which you would like to have lost that 5kg from your tummy, hips and thighs?

Prospect- Yep I am going on holidays in 3 months

SALES: Great! And how often do you think you would like to train to ensure you lose that 5kg? **(TRAIN)**

Prospect – a couple of times a week

SALES: Fantastic Emily! If you enjoyed your training here and could see yourself losing the 5kg through our training programs – would you consider continuing training after the 5 days (assuming we have given them a 5/7 day pass at outreach)? **(QUALIFY)**

Prospect – Yes/maybe

SALES: Great Emily! We can certainly help you out with losing those 5kg from your tummy, hips and thighs so you are feeling great come time for your holiday in 3 months! I'd love to meet up with you so we can Call further about helping you out, so all we need to do is organise a time for you to come down to the club, will you be training in the mornings or afternoons/evenings?

Prospect – after work/evening

SALES: Ok great! Let's catch up either tonight or tomorrow night?

Prospect – tonight

SALES: Fantastic, what's better for you – 5:40 pm or 6:20pm?

Prospect – 6:20pm

SALES: Ok we are _____, so just next to_____do you know where that is?

Prospect – yes!

*always use a landmark where possible to clearly demonstrate the location

SALES: If you need to reach me or make any changes, just call me on _____

SALES: Emily, I have found that most members tend to be more successful achieving their results by training with others (it keeps them motivated!) and we would love to extend the visit to a friend or family member – who would you like to bring down with you?

moreclientslesswork.com

Prospect – Ok I'll bring my sister (get their name) If they don't have anyone to bring ("if you think of anyone feel free to bring them along tomorrow night and you can have a workout together)

SALES: Great to Call to you today Emily. Have an awesome day today and I'm really looking forward to helping you tomorrow and putting a results plan together so you are ready for your holiday!

REACTIVATION SCRIPT

SALES: Hi (ex-member), this is Jade from Business Health Clubs Melbourne, how are you today?

Prospect – well thanks

SALES: Great! I thought I would give you a quick call to let you know about a special promotion we have this week for our members that have taken a break from their training with us, you still live in the Brunswick area (ex-member)? **(LIVE)**

Prospect – Yes I do

SALES: Well, we are giving away (promotion) to all our renewing members who make a positive change to their health and fitness, how good is that?

Prospect – great

SALES: Are you happy with your health and fitness at the moment Pele?

Prospect – answer

SALES: Ok, if you were to start your training again, what would you want to do; some cardio, weights, classes?

Prospect – answer

SALES: Ok by doing (cardio/classes weights –what they have said) what's your number one priority? Is it toning, trimming, building, and strengthening? **(RESULTS)**

SALES: Ok, where are some parts of your body you're not happy with that you want to (insert goals – tone/trim etc.) from?

Prospect – answer

SALES: Why is it important for you Pele to (build up in your upper body?)

Prospect – answer

ENSURE THAT YOU DO NOT MOVE ON UNTIL YOU HAVE THE PAIN. Other questions to use where the opportunity presents itself are:

- How is that a problem for you?
- How does not having that strength in your upper body make you feel?

moreclientslesswork.com

SALES: Do you have something special coming up for which you would like to have gained that strength and muscle in your upper body?

SALES: Do you have something special coming up for which you would like to have lost that 5kg from your tummy, hips and thighs?

Prospect- Yep I am going on holidays in 3 months

SALES: Great! And how often do you think you would like to train to ensure you build that upper boys strength before your holidays? **(TRAIN)**

Prospect – a couple of times a week

SALES: Great (ex-member)! We can certainly help you out with building that upper body strength so you are feeling great come time for your holiday in 3 months! I'd love to meet up with you so we can Call further about helping you out, so all we need to do is organise a time for you to come down to the club, will you be training in the mornings or afternoons/evenings?

Prospect – after work/evening

SALES: Ok great! Let's catch up either tonight or tomorrow night?

Prospect – tonight

SALES: Fantastic, what's better for you – 5:40 pm or 6:20pm?

Prospect – 6:20pm

SALES: Ok we are _____, so just next to_____do you know where that is?

Prospect – yes!

always use a landmark where possible to clearly demonstrate the location

SALES: If you need to reach me or make any changes, just call me on

_____

SALES: (Ex-member), I have found that most members tend to be more successful achieving their results by training with others (it keeps them motivated!) and we would love to extend the visit to a friend or family member – who would you like to bring down with you?

NO-SHOW TO APPOINTMENT

SALES: Hi Lance, this is Jade from Business Health Clubs Perth, how are you today?

Prospect – answer

SALES: Great! I thought I wold give you a call to make sure everything was ok? As we were supposed to catch up on_____to discuss (re-cap the prospects goals and pain)

Prospect – oh, sorry about that…

SALES: No worries – so everything is ok?

Prospect – answer

SALES: Ok, well obviously achieving _____(goals) was important to you when we spoke last, I'm guessing that it is still important to you?

Prospect – answer

SALES: Great! Well given that it is, let's make another time to Call and put together a results plan for you to achieve (goals) you'll be right to make it in?

Prospect – answer

SALES: Ok – you said you would be training (after work) so would tonight or tomorrow night suit you better?

Prospect – answer

SALES: Great, tonight –I have space at 6:20 or 7:15 better for you?

Prospect – answer

SALES: As we mentioned the other day, most people are more motivated training with a friend – who would you like to bring?

Prospect – answer

SALES: No worries Lance! I have put some information together regarding your goals – and looking forward to helping you out tomorrow!!

FOLLOW UP NOT JOINED

SALES: Hey Jemma, this is Jade calling from Business health clubs at Sydney(location), how are you today?

Prospect – answer

SALES: Great! I thought I would give you a call after we spoke about (re-cap the prospects needs and pain) but you couldn't get started yet because_____(insert objection), wasn't it?

Prospect – answer

SALES: Well, I know you were excited about losing that weight (or insert specific goals), have you done anything about achieving that yet?

Prospect – answer

SALES: Ok, if there was absolutely nothing stopping you from losing that weight for your holiday (or insert other goals and timeframes), when would you look at getting started?

Prospect – answer

SALES: If that's the case, let's catch up again and I will Call to my manager to see if we can fix what it is that is stopping you from getting started ok?

Prospect – answer

SALES: Ok, let's catch up either tonight or tomorrow night?

Prospect – answer

SALES: Have you found someone to train with to bring with you tomorrow night – so you can both stay motivated?

Prospect – answer

SALES: No worries Jemma, Have a great day, I look forward to helping you out and getting you started with your training – bring you work out gear so you can also have a workout tomorrow night and get straight into (achieving your goals!)

Be our guest

Face to Face

And now the moment of magic. Who feels most at home in front of people? Or does it scare you? Do you need to put it on? Yeah, you need to put it on. Like the old adage fake it until you make it. Because perception is reality. Alright enough clichés let's get in front of people, where; the game is on.

A chance to connect, to meet, to build rapport, find mutual commonality, to find out goals, to meet their needs. For them to find their answer in your experience and passion. I don't know about you, but this is where the fun begins. My goal is always to make people feel like;

They are in the right place at the right time

Does your experience make them feel this way? Like a guest in your home, like they are meant to be here and they couldn't have chosen a better time. My encouragement to you is be ready, be there in the moment, like they are the only person in this world. Greet them like you have been looking forward to seeing them all day… perhaps you have? Smile, make eye-contact, introduce yourself, ask about their name (if you don't already know it). Greet with a handshake.

We can follow an American based system called 10-10-10, meaning

First 10 feet – 10 feet away looking and smiling at them

First 10 inches – Fresh breath, well groomed, great greeting

First 10 seconds – Ask genuine questions and give them a snapshot of what will happen today

I always, a personal favourite is to make them laugh, or at least laugh at myself. Take them to a place they would feel comfortable in and if the opportunity allows offer them refreshment. Once we have done this we are ready and positioned to find out all about them and their needs.

How do you like to make people feel like they are in the right place at the right time?

_____

_____

_____

_____

_____

_____

Needs analysis for health club prospect

Information to consider;

Can be an internal Needs analysis document or PC based program, this is your info gathering tool.

Typically ask them questions in line with my suggested Needs Analysis tool, found in my toolkit.

Spend 5 minutes here and find 2 things in common. We call this mutual commonality.

The SALES person should spend at least 20 seconds looking at their information, looking over the prospective members details and building rapport. Pay attention to;

- Recognizing that it is their birthday or that they just had one.
- Acknowledging that they work for one of our corporate partners.
- Recognizing the member that referred them.
- Walk in greeting or Booked appointment greeting

OUTLINE of questions to be included in typical needs analysis

We'd like to know more about your goals and what motivates you

Are you currently exercising?

_____

"Do you remember a time when you felt the best you have ever been or better than you do now? When was that? What were you doing? How many times per week? What did you enjoy? Tell me about the results you achieved? Etc. How did you feel back then? How did you look back then?

So I know how fit you were back then, on a scale of 0 to 10, with 10 being the best you could ever be & 0 the worst, where were you then?(y) where are you now? (x)And where do you want to get to, is it between (x) & (y), back to (y) or beyond (y)?"

Have you been a member of a health club before?
_____

How did you find it? What did you like? What didn't you enjoy?

What do you need to see with us?

What motivated you to get started today?
_____

Great well I'm glad you chosen Business, we are happy to see how Business Fits with You.

How long have you been thinking about getting started...?
_____

Really that seems like a while, tell me what's been going through your mind for (period of time)?

OK so is (period of time) a long enough time to be thinking about getting started?

Great, well I'm glad you've stopped thinking about it, you made tha hard step getting down here, it gets a whole lot easier from here.

What are you Main Goals? – Movement towards pleasure

This section should be both visual and auditory, by simply getting the member to point or circle the areas that they would like to focus on gives them ownership of their goals.
Finding out how important these goals are and when they want to achieve them will give the SALES invaluable information when handling objections.
Clearly identify the needs that the prospect wants to work on and when. Eg. Do you want to achieve these results by Christmas or Easter? Great! Get the prospective member to buy into a time frame.(Xmas)
Then, ask the question: Would you be interested in finding out a way to FAST TRACK your results?

What are your goals – avoidance of pain
4W'S & H – This is the most important section

There are a number of goals here that you can achieve, which ones are important to you?
What is your number 1 priority? (write #1 next to it)
Where are the 3 main areas you are not happy with? (circle areas and write the names they call them)
Why these areas, what don't you like about them?
When do you want to achieve these results by? (once set a date, ask detailed questions about what they are doing, etc. to paint a visual picture in their minds of the event)
OR   When would be the last date you could handle being in this current condition?
What do you think you need to do to ensure this happens?

      OK, so you are ready to make those changes then?
      You are in a position to get started?
How would you feel come this date & you haven't changed your exercise program, so you are still feeling that your arms are too flabby & your belly hangs over you jeans (if that is what they have told you in the first 3 W's above) how would that affect your holiday/birthday/wedding? (whatever the goal date was for).

Does that worry you? _____ Why?

Rescue:

So you're going to do something about it?   You're going to make some changes?

Nothing's going to get in your way?

Well I'm glad you've made that decision, you've done the hard part getting down here, it gets a whole lot easier from here.

OR   Well that's ok, you said you are coming in 4*/week so that will have you well on your way to looking fantastic with toned arms & belly for your holiday in December" (again, all things the client has told you from above).

Linking in

How do you feel about your current fitness? (1 to 10)_____

OK, so you like to maintain or improve that feeling?
When did you feel your best or better than you do now?
What was different then, what were you doing?   How often?
How did you feel back then?   How did you look?

What do you feel has prevented you from getting started? (list objections)

_____

So given that you've said you are gonna make some changes and nothing is going to get in your way, it would be safe to say we are not going to let (objection) _____ get in your way?

Great well I'm glad you've made that decision, nothing will hold you back then?

Is this still a problem?

No – Great I'm glad it's not still a problem and you have decided to do something about it

Yes – Well given that you mentioned you were ready to make some changes is it safe to say that you are not going to let any problems hold you back?

How many times per week will you need to train to achieve your results? _____

OK, so you are going to commit to this so you can achieve your goals?

Goals are nothing without follow through, if you can commit to achieving your goals, write them down and have someone support you to achieving your goals. You've taken the hardest step.

What are the main areas you would love to train in?

_____

(This is your tour plan, hot spot.)

Sounds good, shall we go have a look at the club?

Tour

Taking the prospect through your facility or services

Important things to mention when on the tour:
When stopping at the PT Board mention that "most members have a personal trainer!"
"You were looking at Kick starting your results weren't you?"
All of our trainers are fully qualified and as you can see they specialise in different fields."

Feature, Benefit, Emotion Agreement (FBEA)

E.G: "This is the (cardio area). This is where you will be exercising with other people similar to yourself in a fun & motivating environment to (reduce your body fat), which will allow you to feel (really comfortable in that formal dress at your birthday), which is what you are after isn't it?" (positive NLP).

At least 3 FBEA's per tour all directly relating to the information they told you in their NEEDS ANALYSIS.

Transition questions:
"Is there anything in the Club that you want to see but have not, or does it suit you perfectly?
So you can see yourself exercising with us can't you? (Positive NLP)
Apart from affordability, do you have any other questions?
Let me show you how easy it is to get started?"

Timeline

"What I would like to do is take you through a timeline of what your body will go through as you start exercising with us. There are 3 stages you will go through.
Today you mentioned you are a 4 out of 10 and you would like to get to a 10/10 was it?

Your plan of action was to;
Do cardio 1x week?
RPM on Thurs night?
Weights with Sam(example friend's name)?
And cut down on those tim tams?

The first is the feel stage, where you will meet your trainer & they will design your program & show you how to use the equipment. You will start to do your group fitness classes you mentioned & come in those 3 times per week. You will feel an increase in energy, a decrease in toxins & an increase in your quality of sleep.
Then you will enter the see stage, which is the most exciting stage. It is where you will notice you are stronger & recovering easier, you will notice a change in the way your clothes fit, how the mirror looks back at you & the positive feedback you will get from family & friends, particularly in your arms, stomach & legs that are important to you (the areas the prospect mentioned in 4w's & h).
From there, you will move to the maintain stage where you keep all the great results you have achieved. Once you achieve these results, how long do you want to keep them for? (Circle & tick maintain stage when they answer "forever or similar").

The top line here represents the results you will achieve with results based training and below the results you will get training on your own. You mentioned you want to fast track your results and maintain them long term didn't you? (Positive NLP*). So, you can see the benefits of the **results based training** can't you?"

Pass – Well *"14 days"* only gets you to here, what we will do is trade that in and give you the first *"14 days"* on your membership and move you to maintain it forever where you really want to get to.

NLP stands for Neuro Linguistic Programming – Google it

VIP GUEST LIST – script

The great news about becoming a member is – you can add your 5 of your friends and family members to our VIP guest list (just like at a night club)– if they are on our guest list that means that can come in for a workout and won't have to pay the $20! Which is great isn't? Just think of friends and family (isolating faces e.g. work/school/sport etc) that live close and would be interested in getting started on some training! I'll leave this with you!

REFERRAL PROGRAM SCRIPT

The following offers are suggested and you can choose what meets your needs

Congratulations on getting started today! This is the final piece of paperwork we need to complete today – we find that most members train more often and get their results quicker if they have someone to train with – thus, why we are so excited about giving you the Business Gold Pass today! The Gold Pass entitles you to bring any family member or friend with you for free to every workout for the next 30 days!

The other great part for you is - we have a program whereby, every time you introduce a new member to the Business – you benefit!

If one of your friends gets started– you're entitled to a Business member pack!

If you have a second friend that gets started – you receive a month free on your membership!

If a THIRD friend gets started – you receive ANOTHER month for free and a free PT session!

Which is awesome isn't it?

moreclientslesswork.com

All you need to do for you to qualify for the program is – just have a think about your friends and family they may want to come down and train with you – jot them on the list – that way if they get started we can register them against your membership and you will benefit with all the Business goodies! I'll leave that with you whilst I get your new member pack!

Referrals at Point Of Sale

Trainer to role-play the entire process considering;

Body position in relation to member

No distractions, only referrals in front of member, no other merchandise

'Chunk' referral training

Demonstrate each chunk then get SALESs to role-play twice each

Do chunk 1 then 1 and 2 then 1,2 and 3 etc.

Chunk 1

'First of all let's start with these, which is a gift to you as a new member!'

'These are 6 trial passes for your friends, family or work colleagues'

'The passes are worth $20 each, that's $120 in total!'

'Because these are yours I'll get you to pop your name and number down here'

Chunk 2

'And just the names and numbers of the 6 friends you like to invite down'

'I'll get you to do that for me now, I'll be a few minutes on the computer…'

Turn to the computer and start entering in their details

Chunk 3

If member is having difficulty putting down names

'So who have we nominated so far?' – *listen to response*

'What most people do is scroll through their mobile to invite down friends'

'You'll probably find 20 people, but I can only give you 6.'

Reposition page in front of them to try again

Chunk 4

'Thanks for that; you let your friends know you have invited them down

and I'll give them a call to invite them down as your guest'

Other ways to generate referrals

When making every appointment, ask <u>**who**</u> would you like to bring with you?

SALES - Most people train with a friend, **who** would you like to bring with you?

PROSPECT – Oh, I can't think of anyone.

SALES – OK, most people invite their best friend, how about a family member or your best friend?

PROSPECT – yeah ok my best mate

SALES – And their name is? And their number?

Someone says no to an appointment

> Well it is a free trial valued at $20, I'd hate for it to go to waste, if you can't use it, **who** would you like to pass it on to?

Reception

> Have you entered the competition yet? – No –

> It's great it's to win <insert referral prize here> simply pop your name here
> (pass referral slip)

> And the name and number of your best friend. (once they start filling it out)

> Great and perhaps, your mum and dad and some other friends, the more you enter the more chance there is of winning.

I have made it is easy as possible to average over 3 per sale because all service call referrals go to your average and I expect 3 just from POS. You can do it!

Feedback and questions – consider when training

What went well, in relation to scripting

Areas to improve on

Explain the 'why' it is done in this manner

- Referrals are immeasurable in worth to the business
- They have a track record of giving SALESs better %s
- It is an effective manner of prospecting
- We can mathematically work out how many referrals required to run your entire business from referrals
- No time or less time wasted collecting leads from lead boxes and other sources
- Warmer call than a cold call as we already know of the prospect
- We are offering a service to the referrer as they will have a chance to train with someone else

Ask if there are any questions

Ask is this helpful, reconfirm any training needs

Accountability

We will role-play the entire process in tomorrow's 10 minute SALES meeting

I will check up with you at 1 week to monitor improvement and then again in 2 weeks to celebrate the wins (or times specified in outcomes expected)

Check stats to see improvement in % and see the benefit of it for the SALES

Close

Outcomes of what is expected, set a goal and achieve this week, monitor your progress.

If you can't measure it, you can't manage it

More Clients
Less Work

Problem Isolation
and
Solution Charts

Low Appointment Ratio

	Reason	Suggested course of action
1	Not closing for the appointment	Ensure alternate choice question being used.
2	Poor quality leads	Review lead base. Review new business generation strategies. Focus on
3	Not using scripts	Role play phone scripts.
4	Poor skill levels on particular types of calls	Analyse specific types of calls causing problems.
5	No urgency	Create urgency. Ensure alternate choice question being used. Refer to Sales
6	Not taking control by asking questions	Role play phone scripts. Refer to Sales Scripts
7	Poor rapport building	Role play phone scripts. Refer to Sales Scripts
8	Lack of enthusiasm/excitement/passion	Role play phone scripts. Add fun factor into the boiler room. Ensure
9	Aggressive tone being used	Role play more appropriate delivery style.
10	Giving prices over the phone	Refer to phone in script
11	Giving all facility details over the phone	Refer to phone in script
12	Counting leads as contacts	Clearly define what is a contact and what is a lead

13	Phoning too long without a break	When it's HOT keep calling, when it's not go for a walk
15	Unorganised. No specific planned time for specific calls	During daily catch up make sure structured call times are planned and
16	Ghosting contacts	Manager to follow up leads to check for discrepancies

Low Show Ratio

	Reason	Suggested course of action
1	Poor quality leads	Review lead base. Review new business generation strategies. Focus on
2	Poor rapport building before making appointments	Role play phone scripts. Refer to Sales Scripts – build need, ALF
3	SALES forcing the appointment. No value created	Build need, ALF - Role play phone scripts. Refer to Sales Scripts
4	Incomplete appointments. No specific time and date	If a specific time and date does not exist then it's not an appointment!
5	Counting reschedules as appointments	Rescheduled appointments are not to be counted as
6	Appointments set more than 48 hours in advance	Only count appointments set for next 2 working days.
7	Counting groups as multiple appointments	Couples/groups to be counted as 1 appointment not as multiple
8	Poor confirmation script	Role play confirmation script. Refer to Sales Scripts
9	Lack of enthusiasm/excitement/passion	Role play phone scripts. Add fun factor into the boiler room. Ensure belief
10	Giving prices over the phone	Refer to phone in script
11	Giving all facility details over the phone	Refer to phone in script

12	Low skill level dealing with certain types of leads	Analyse specific types of calls causing problems. Refer to Sales Scripts
13	Weather conditions/sporting or special events/school holidays/etc	Plan ahead where possible. Activity targets need to be set higher to
14	Facility location	Emphasize clear directions when making appointments
15	Ghosting of appointments	Manager to confirm appointments

Low Presentation to Referral Ratio

	Reason	Suggested course of action
1	Not asking for referrals	SALES must ask from every sale! Referral sheets to be easily accessible to presentation area. Role play referral script. Refer
2	Fear of asking for referrals	Role play referral script. Refer to Sales Scripts
3	Poor referral closing skills	Role play referral script. Refer to Sales Scripts
4	Allowing the member to take the guest passes home	Do not allow this practice to occur! They complete then give to SALES
5	Not using/ understanding the current referral deal	Role play the current referral deal. Refer to Sales Scripts or launch document
6	Poor rapport building throughout presentations	Role play presentations. Refer to Sales Scripts
7	SALES doesn't believe in referrals	SALES needs to overcome personal beliefs about referrals and ASSUME that members will nominate referrals when given the opportunity in the correct
8	SALES doesn't understand the benefits to the member when they nominate friends as referrals	Review the benefits of referrals to the members (training partner, better exercise adherence, etc) Refer to Sales
9	SALES not confident with calling referrals	Role play referral script. Refer to Sales Scripts

Low Close Ratio

	Reason	Suggested course of action
1	Not using NEEDS ANALYSIS	Ensure NEEDS ANALYSIS is delivered at all presentations
2	Tour performed before doing 4Ws and a H	Follow selling cycle – rapport building, 4Ws and a H
3	Poor introduction	Make a friend, make them smile, 10-10-10
4	Poor rapport	Role play use of NEEDS ANALYSIS, Domino or ALF based questioning
5	Not overcoming objections prior to tour	Overcome objections as they come up, before price presentation
6	Tour too long	It's about needs not facilities
7	The price is perceived as too high by SALES	Value for money, reduction to the ridiculous, hello people buy cigarettes!
8	Timeline not done	Do it – role play scripts Trade in pass on the timeline
9	Fear of closing asking for money	Close all the time, not on price. Lower buyer's resistance, don't sell
10	SALES not aware of close techniques	Refer to overcoming objections, role play

11	Problem creating excitement/ urgency	FVI – if you don't today, you never will
12	Poor presentation skills	Role play until you can say scripts backwards

"Remember, the secret to selling is 'sincerity' ... once you can fake that you've got it made."

Resources and reference materials can be found at;

www.moreclientslesswork.com
Including; Sales tools for your business needs

Sales Manuals to follow
Create more leads where people want to buy

Stop wasting opportunities and start gaining happy clients

Remove the fear of closing the sale
If you don't do it, someone else will

WHY WE SELL	REMOVE OBJECTIONS
HOW TO SELL	COMMUNICATION
LEAD GENERATION	SALES SCRIPTS

Tools to develop your business

GymSales.net	Online Lead management system
NLP	Neuro Linguistic Programming
NPS	Net Promoter Score

About Me

Jade Philippe is Building Better Business, by creating **More Clients for Less Work**.
I am passionate about health and fitness businesses and seeing them successful.
After working with a range of large and small health clubs and PT studios I know the good times and hurdles we face. Learn from others mistakes and build on your successes.
Together we can Build Better Business and get More Clients for Less Work.

- Create Sales - Procedures to sales process automation
- Execution of best practice sales process
- Sales manuals - how to guide e-book
- Sales scripting - take away the guess work e-book
- Massive action sales impact
- Improvement in major Key Performance Indicators
- Business consulting
- Lead to sale execution

Jade Philippe
More Clients for Less Work

Get Leads, Boost Sales and Retain Clients

0403 070 031
jade.philippe@mail.com
moreclientslesswork.com